June
2000

Happy
Birthday
Michele —
may this gift bring
you pleasure and —
inspire you creatively
whether in your garden or
exploring different art media.

Love,
Theo

THE color GARDEN

(red)

THE

color

GARDEN

(red)

single color plantings
for dramatic landscapes

TEXT & PHOTOGRAPHY BY ELVIN MᶜDONALD
INTRODUCTION BY BRIDE M. WHELAN

CollinsPublishersSanFrancisco
A Division of HarperCollinsPublishers

A Packaged Goods Incorporated Book

First published 1995 by
Collins Publishers San Francisco
1160 Battery Street
San Francisco, CA 94111-1213

Conceived and produced by
Packaged Goods Incorporated
9 Murray Street, New York, NY 10007
A Quarto Company

Design by Stephen Fay
Endpapers by Michael Levine
Series Editor: Kristen Schilo

Seeds © Copyright 1995 White Swan Ltd., Beaverton, OR. White Swan® and Garden Accents® are registered trademarks of White Swan Ltd.

McDonald, Elvin.
    The color garden (red) : single color plantings for dramatic
landscapes / text & photographs by Elvin McDonald.
        p.   cm.
    Includes Index.
    ISBN 0-00-225075-6
    1. Red gardens.   I. Title.
SB454.3.C64M38 1995
635.9'68—dc20   94-37918
                                                               CIP

Seed packet photo by Environmental Seed Producers
Color separations by Wellmak Printing Press Limited
Printed and bound in Hong Kong by Sing Cheong Printing Co. Ltd.

10 9 8 7 6 5 4 3 2 1

red's for courage
and sweet William

Thanks especially to the gardeners who permitted me to photograph in their gardens...

Ron and Don Bayer, Houston, TX; Big Thicket National Reserve, East Texas; Philip Bondi, Western Pennsylvania; Bourton House, England; W. Atlee Burpee Co., Warminster, PA; Butchart Gardens, Victoria, B.C., Canada; Columbus Park of Roses, Columbus, OH; Cooks Garden, Londonderry, VT; Cranford Rose Garden, Brooklyn Botanic Garden, Brooklyn, NY; The Stuart Crowners, Pasadena, CA; The James Daduras, Houston, TX; Dixon Gallery and Gardens, Memphis, TN; The Farm, Nelsonville, TX; The Garden Club of Houston; Golden Gate Park Conservatory, San Francisco, CA; Goldsmith Seeds, Gilroy, CA; Hope Hendler, New York, NY; Hortus Bulborum, The Netherlands; Huntsville (AL) Botanic Garden; Jardins des Plantes, Paris, France; Lauray of Salisbury, Salisbury, CT; Leonardslee Gardens, England; Lilypons Water Gardens, Brookshire, TX; Christopher Lloyd's gardens at Great Dixter, England; Logee's Greenhouses, Danielson, CT; Manito Park Conservatory and Gardens, Spokane, WA; Mr. and Mrs. David B. Martin, Memphis, TN; Mercer Arboretum & Botanic Garden, Humble, TX; Mohonk Mountain House, New Paltz, NY; Moody Gardens, Galveston, TX; The New York Botanical Garden, Bronx, NY; Geo. W. Park Seed Co., Inc., Greenwood, SC; Mr. and Mrs. Dave Pendarvis, Lake Charles, LA; Phipps Conservatory, Pittsburgh, PA; Pier 39, San Francisco, CA; Plum Creek Farm, Sharon, CT; The Forum of the River Oaks Garden Club, Houston, TX; Rosedown Plantation, St. Francisville, LA; Royal Botanical Gardens at Kew, London, England; Shady Hill Gardens, Batavia, IL; Sir John Thouron, Unionville, PA; Cornelus Warmenhoven, The Netherlands; The Wayside Gardens Co., Hodges, SC.

🌿 Heirloom garden pinks such
as Dianthus 'Pretty Dottie' have
been popular garden flowers
since the 1600s.

contents

introduction

The focal color of nature is red, and by itself, it is a pivotal garden color. Red defines and fills any space, large or small, with a vivid and unforgettable palette. A garden filled to abundance with blooming red plants and flowers is exciting, powerful, and grand.

A single-color garden is a form of balance and harmony. In order to duplicate nature's balanced contrast of light and shadow, a monochromatic garden needs careful planning. The harmony which counterpoints this contrast is achieved through simplicity and repetition. Red, at the center of the colorwheel, has as its neighbors blue-violet and red-violet on its cool side and red-orange and orange on its warm side. When a grouping of any three of these hues, with their tints and shades of pink, violet, salmon, pale orange, burgundy, and terra cotta, are translated into a floral bed or order, the striking result is an array of tulips, *(page 10)* or sweet William *(pages 12-13)*, extraordinary in their intensity and vibrance. Verdant background shades, from mint to hunter green, are the perfect complement to red and balance this blazing color feast.

Reds, vermilions, and magentas advance toward the eye and send a hot and sultry message throughout the flowering season. A vivid bed of red-orange poppies is an example of flowers not diminished by other reds of the garden; they instead play off the strengths of the parent hue. Magenta or red-violet, a prominent member of the red family, has a blue undertone and is complemented by varieties of plants having lime or yellow-green leaves, such as coleus, iresine, and numerous ornamental grasses. When positioned next to true reds, the late-summer maroon of dahlias and chrysanthemums sends a message of smoldering sensuality.

The color red affects the sense of smell, heightening sensitivity, so the heady fragrance of summer is especially strong in a red garden. Beds of spring and summer roses, peonies, and summer phlox seem to have an enhanced odor—a pungent smell with a strong, perfumed sweetness—found only in a garden of red.

Unique and filled with extraordinary beauty, the red garden is not for the timid. If you crave excitement, however, you will not be disappointed; red does it all.

BRIDE M. WHELAN

(I)

b e d s   a n d   b o r d e r s

*R*ED IS ONE OF THE MOST VERSATILE HUES IN THE GARDEN designer's palette, expressing every nuance from the pale innocence of blush pink to the moody mysteries of darkest purple-violet. Between these extremes, plain red is curiously synonymous with stop signs and danger, fiery hot peppers and bull fights, with courage and bravery. No flower save the rose is as evocative of red as the tulip, which appears at the beginning of a new gardening season when all colors are freshest, cleanest, and most welcome.

Gardeners often underplant tulips with English daisies, wallflowers, forget-me-nots, pansies, or violets, in the same or in complementary colors. Monet, the French Impressionist painter, was thought daring at the beginning of the 20th century when he set together tulips that were bright pink, cherry-red, and purple.

Reds that scintillate can be
found in most gardens
nearly every day of the year.
Red-twig dogwood
streaks the landscape through
coldest winter, followed
by nesting cardinals, demure
English daisies, brash
and bold sweet Williams
(right). Summer in hot
places is made bearable by
the bodacious oleander
(above) and fall brings in the
glory days for red leaves.

Red tulips and blue forget-me-nots *(Myosotis palustris)* salute spring in a bed hedged by dwarf boxwood at Jardins des Plantes in Paris. When the tulips finish, they might be succeeded by red hybrid bedding geraniums *(Pelargonium)*, large red zinnias, or a variety of different sages *(Salvia)* having red flowers in summer. A strong candidate for red beginning midsummer and continuing through frost is the red dahlia in many sizes.

Large-flowered hybrid zinnias like 'Sun Red' *(above)* celebrate the cheeriest of colors. Their simplicity and summer flowering suit them to porch pots and cottage gardens.

Dwarf boxwoods outline parterre beds that showcase different plantings each season: pink and orange lily-flowered tulips or hyacinths in spring, pink and orange impatiens in summer and fall. On occasion in winter this latticed city backyard is blanketed with snow. White gravel carpets the surrounding walk.

Obedience plant *(Physostegia virginiana)* grows knee high, with spikes of rose-purple flowers (white in the *alba* variety and 'Summer Snow'); a strong and spreading perennial in compost-enriched, moist, well-drained soil and lots of sun...whose natural color range is from white to the glowing rose-purple seen here (and photographed in the East Texas Big Thicket)...Mix or match with snapdragons and daylilies, Shasta daisies and blue echinops.

Red pansies (*Viola* x *wittrockiana*) and violas (*V. cornuta*) come in the rich colors of Oriental rugs. There is the ruby-red of yellow-eyed 'Arkwright Ruby,' a viola that mixes smartly with the buttery spring yellows...jonquils, small daffodils...or can be matched with tulips, wallflowers, English daisies...or red Japanese mustard greens in a salad patch. Pansies come in scarlet, mahogany, purple, rose, bronze, carmine, brick red, rose, and pink.

Today's petunias, both vivid and subdued, hardly hint at their forebears whose flowers ranged in a muddled way from dull white to purplish-red magenta. In the right place at the right season, there is nothing in the color garden so facile as the petunia...reds so red they defy description, some veering toward orange, others toward blue. Pinks and purples pale or darken similarly.

Hardy asters and the taller-growing dahlias from tubers (instead of the short seed-grown annual types) are flowers that glory in the cool, crisp weather of autumn. Dahlias are strong in red, from bluish to orangey, paling through all the pinks and salmons, to creamy and snowy whites. Fall asters may be ruby-red, violet-red, lavender, blue, or white; the dwarfs are just right for bed edgers, the taller ones perfect height for dahlia mingling.

🐚 Silvery pink tulips curve
gracefully from a clear glass vase.
They last longest in cool
temperatures and water that is
refreshed daily.

One incentive for cultivating a monochromatic flower garden is to produce an abundance of cut flowers for the house, for rooms where their color is critical to achieving a desired effect. Some outstanding sources for reds and pinks include tulips, roses, carnations, and other dianthus, dahlias, zinnias, and snapdragons. All of these are found nearly year 'round in the cut flower market, and all are suited to growing efficiently in a home garden having well-drained soil and a half day or more of sun.

🌿 'Alabama Red' coleus *(above)*, developed for growing in the sun, runs the gamut from coral, to red, to bronze, depending on sun strength and temperatures.

🐚 Coral hemerocallis *(near right)* and 'Camano Peach' dahlia *(far right)* complement purples such as heliotrope and tibouchina.

The fire pink (*Silene virginica*) blooms its clusters of purplish, red, or scarlet flowers over a long season, beginning in spring and continuing until early autumn. Like fire pink, *Phlox drummondii (left)*, is at its best when set free in a wild garden, or encouraged to colonize a sandy bank, alone or with friendly red companions... verbena, scarlet pimpernel *(Anagallis arvensis)*, standing cypress *(Ipomopsis rubra)*, and Texas sage *(Salvia coccinea)*.

Or try the *Phlox drummondii* interplanted with lavender-blue 'Baby Lucia,' a miniature, true pansy that self-sows.

🐛 Two vivids make one dramatic combination *(left):* painted daisy *(Chrysanthemum coccineum)* and sea pink *(Armeria maritima).* 'Sensation' cosmos *(above, upper)* and 'Pink Panther' catharanthus *(above, lower)* run the red range from palest pink to intense crushed-berry reds and purples. Mix with compatible blues.

For containers and tropical gardens: 'Barbara Karst' bougainvillea blooms are close to the same red (with a hint of blue) that is used in the four-color printing process.

"Bright red" at first impression may reveal at second glance a bluish coolness or, conversely, sunny warmth. The papery, flower-like bracts of 'Barbara Karst' bougainvillea are an example of a highly visible red with traces of blue or cyanine, the result being what is known universally in color printing as "process red." Bougainvilleas that have more blue in the red are seen as bluish- or rose-pink while those with more yellow may suggest orange, copper, or salmon-pink. These clambering shrubs or vines from the tropics can be managed as container plants in cold climates, placed outdoors in full sun in warm weather, and kept inside, frost-free and on the dry side, in winter.

Summer phlox (*Phlox paniculata*) occurs wild in Eastern North America, to as far south as Georgia. The usual color is a pale to deep magenta. The hybrids tell another story: reds ('Starfire,' *opposite*), pinks, oranges, lavenders, and purples of extraordinary hue, the glory of a summer flower garden. Hardly anything that can be cut from a garden seems so bounteous (and uniquely scented for bouquet making). The drawbacks are powdery mildew later on ('Bright Eyes,' florets soft pink with a red eye, is notably disease-resistant) and unsuitability for warm, frost-free climates. More than two dozen named cultivars are available, so that subtle colorations and varying habits can be woven into the garden picture.

(2)

c o n t a i n e r s

$\mathcal{R}$ED FLOWERS ARE SYNONYMOUS WITH CONTAINER GARDENS: winter and spring pots of red tulips and rosy carmine hyacinths, followed by roses and all manner of geraniums, those whose real name is *Pelargonium*, such as 'Red Comet' *(above)*, to carry through until winter when amaryllis of the clan *Hippeastrum* put on a major show of trumpet flowers. At any season the velvety florist gloxinia *(Sinningia)* can be a cheering presence, not to mention holiday poinsettia *(Euphorbia pulcherrima)*, Christmas and Easter cacti *(Schlumbergera* and *Rhipsalidopsis gaertneri)*, and kalanchoes, available year-round, in hot or cool reds.

Potted red-and-white parrot tulips *(opposite)* make any doorway or garden gate exciting. To enjoy the longest season, select different types of red tulips—from the earliest species and doubles to the latest cottage and Rembrandts.

🌿 'Lilac Mist' is a Deacon-type *Pelargonium*, bred by an English minister. The double rose-pink flowers appear freely in winter on compact floribunda bushes.

🌿 'Rose Lady' belongs to the Painted Lady class of *Pelargonium*; exceptionally large flower trusses are pink-red with white.

🌿 'Skelly's Pride' is a carnation-flowered *Pelargonium* in dark salmon-orange, noted for floral abundance.

A foremost showplace in the world to see *Hippeastrum* like this smartly bicolored red-and-white holiday amaryllis, is at the Queen's Pavilion in Keukenhof, the Netherlands' fabled bulb display gardens outside Amsterdam, at Lisse.

The only true *Amaryllis* in cultivation is the South African *A. belladona*, which sends up scapes of rose- to pale- or bluish-pink flowers in early fall, after the leaves have died. It combines well with pink-to-blue ageratums and dwarf asters. Most of the plants grown around the world and called amaryllis belong to the South American genus *Hippeastrum*. The large-flowered hybrids come mostly from Dutch breeders, Warmenhoven, for example, whose handiwork is seen opposite in a display for the Queen's Pavilion at Keukenhof gardens situated in the heart of the bulb growing district around Lisse, and at right in the family greenhouses at Hillegom.

At the end of the 20th century there is a trend among breeders toward creating much smaller flowered *Hippeastrum* plants that can form clumps in a large bulb pan from which dozens of flowers appear together. One of these, 'Scarlet Baby,' is simply redder than red, a winter garden's brightest hope.

The amaryllis of the trade name seems designed by nature to travel, so it is no wonder that this bulb is nurtured globally. In milder regions the bulbs can be planted in the ground; they bloom in the spring, around Easter. Where winter means freezing, the bulbs must be brought to cozy warmth in early autumn and kept quite dry until the flowerbuds appear. Then the plants need sun, warmth, water, and fertilizer.

Red ginger (left) is
Alpinia purpurata; pink
ginger is its variety 'Rosea.'
Tropicals from the
South Pacific, they need a
long, warm season for
growing but are available as
long-lasting cut flowers
all year. The shooting-star
florist cyclamen blooms
(above) appear in cool but
frost-free weather; the
plants thrive on buoyant air,
evenly moist soil, and
gentle light.

Fuchsias of all kinds, but especially those with cascading branches, speak their own distinct brand of red, with a particular affinity for out-and-out pinks, purples, and corals, often bi-colored to astounding perfection. Cultivars of *Fuchsia* x *hybrida*, like that shown, grow and bloom spring to fall but are not for summer hot spots. Most heat-tolerant is a hybrid from West Indian stock, 'Gartenmeister Bohnstedt,' the honeysuckle fuchsia, with flowers resembling those in the picture but burgundy-backed leaves.

Fuchsias and cyclamen are two major sources for garden reds during the cooler—but not freezing—growing seasons. While cyclamen are common florist gift plants, often beribboned and foiled to overkill, in many gardens, indoors and out, they are among winter and spring's most cherished flowers, growing luxuriantly in not too much direct sun, almost a cool-season counterpart to impatiens. The plants themselves can be fascinatingly symmetrical, every heart-shaped leaf in place, some merely silver-flecked, others almost entirely metallic. They look especially beautiful in old clay pots and grow best in spacious quarters where the air can circulate freely.

Standard florist and miniature cyclamen have the fortunate habit of blooming into winter and on into late spring or early summer. Fuchsias are more inclined to produce blooms in spring and summer, provided temperatures aren't sweltering. The two make compatible companions at the nursery as well as at home and both are often combined in a complementary way with ferns.

Cyclamen and paper-white narcissus are a natural for winter gardens in pots, or outdoors in the ground where temperatures stay above freezing. Fragrance from narcissus is assumed; some cyclamen also give off a sweet perfume.

(3)

r o s e s   a r e   r e d

ROSES HAVE SET THE STANDARD FOR REDNESS FROM THE beginning of recorded history. Their botanical name, *Rosa*, announces this predilection. There is a rose, antique or modern, for nearly every garden with a half-day of sun or more, in all sizes, from micro-miniatures to arbor-embellishing climbers.

Container-grown roses offered for sale in bloom are the way to pick precise colors, for mixing or matching a well-tuned scheme. At home, it's nice to have roses next to fences, spilling or arching branches around outdoor seating, and fresh cut flowers up close, such as inserted in florist water picks concealed within an evergreen and English ivy door wreath *(above)*. Red and pink roses can be dried, for rich colors in winter arrangements, and some give scent for potpourri.

Roses are among the most sociable of climbers, beautiful in the garden alone or intertwined with clematis, honeysuckle, or jasmine. They are outstanding for all pinks, reds, and oranges, a delightful way to splash color up in the air. Thorns in some roses are red—from pink to glowing burgundy—a trait whose worth becomes evident in winter when the canes are leafless. Cultivated climbing and rambling roses— representing two distinct classes— are just right for embellishing fences, trellises, arbors, and walls. Roses shown are 'Showbiz' floribunda *(near right, upper)*, 'Curly Pink' hybrid tea *(near right, lower)* in front of *Rosa multiflora*, and 'Excelsa' *(far right)* rambler.

pale pink
(Carla)

is a blush- to salmon-pink hybrid
tea rose that is fragrant and
stands up well in the garden and
as a cut flower. It was introduced
in 1968, from a cross made five
years earlier between 'Queen
Elizabeth' and 'The Optimist.'

mid-pink
(Unforgettable)

is a large-flowered hybrid tea, the
sort of modern rose that is
favored for planting en masse in
formal beds that are framed by
low hedging such as dwarf box
or Yaupon holly. Its coloring is
mid-pink with a silvery luminosity
that moonlight becomes.

dark pink
(Dean Collins)

a grandiflora introduced in 1955,
has unusually large, many-
petaled flowers. This is a fine
example of the many rosebushes
whose new growth shoots are
maroon-red or bronzy, perhaps
most notable in the red-leaved
species, *Rosa rubrifolia*.

pink & white
(Princess de
Monaco)

is a hybrid tea rose introduced in
1981. Besides tea scent and
exquisite conformation, the soft
but distinct mid-pink edging that
details the petals makes this rose
irresistible. It stands up well in
the garden and looks wonderful
indoors, alone in a bud vase or
mixed in a bouquet.

rose pink
(Chestnut rose)

Rosa x roxburghii
was introduced from China to the
West in 1814 and is so-called for
the bristly jackets worn by the
orange-yellow seed hips.
The color of the flowers is bright
pink, with silvery highlights and
hints of blue in aging flowers
seen at twilight.

red red
(Betty Prior)

produces large clusters of single
flowers that are dark carmine-pink,
as many as ten together on the
stem. Introduced in 1938 as one of
the earlier floribundas, 'Betty Prior'
continues to have a devoted follow-
ing. There is no fragrance, but it is
disease-resistant and almost always
in flower, or at least bears red-
peduncled buds showing promise.

The rosarian's year begins with the arrival of catalogs in winter, proceeds to pruning in early spring, and then the fun begins: watching for new growth, the shoots and leaves for much of this time a bronzy red that fairly glows on a sunny day. (Several roses also have thorns that shine ruby-red in winter and spring, most notably 'Red Wing,' whose stems appear almost more winged than thorned.) Next, of course, are the season's first flowers and, for the devotee of red, a protracted visual picnic.

The small bouquets pictured, of antique and modern roses, with the ripe seed hips of species and shrub roses, were actually picked on a December day in the Cranford Rose Garden at the Brooklyn Botanic Garden and photographed to suggest the opulence of color, form, and fragrance at the end of the season. Since even roses that are everblooming stop occasionally to regenerate, the color garden approach makes sense: Plant a variety of different roses, different cultivars, from different classes, all of approximately the same color or color family. The result will be a garden that seems always bursting with blooms.

Rose seed hips are another source of garden color in fall and winter. The birds appreciate them, or if harvested they can be steeped for tea. The colorful hips are also useful for long-lasting bouquets and wreaths.

Small bouquets of old and modern roses mixed with orange and scarlet seed hips from species and shrub roses show how one flower can gracefully embrace at once the cool blue-reds and the warm yellow-reds.

'Climbing First Prize' (overleaf, left) is an ever-blooming, large-flowered climber with bountiful rose-pink blooms that are fragrant. 'New Dawn' is blush pink and tea-scented, an old garden favorite.

Red—or pink—roses and white lattice (overleaf, right) are the stuff of a romantic garden. The lattice supports and backdrops the roses when they are at their best; when not, lattice can be charming unto itself.

Exceptional red roses, that is, red, red roses, include 'Europeana,' 'Mr. Lincoln,' 'Chrysler Imperial,' 'Olympiad,' and 'Taboo' (reddish-black).

(4)

foliage and fruit

ED LEAVES AND FRUIT ALWAYS CELEBRATE LIGHT, BUT NEVER more than on a crisp sunny fall afternoon, after frost or at least some chilly nights have convinced the likes of maples, sourwoods, sweet-gums, beeches, and oaks that the time is near for their transcendence. Earlier in the season there are the red Japanese maple, purple beech, red-leaved Japanese blood grass (*Imperata cylindrica* 'Red Baron'), bronze-purple- leaved *Heuchera micrantha* 'Bressingham Bronze,' and purple-leaved *Ajuga reptans* 'Atropurpurea,' a groundcover.

Finally, into fall and winter, there are the pyracantha and holly berries, orange bittersweet, purple beautyberry, and, a scene best appreciated with snow cover and direct sun: a stand of red-twig dogwood (*Cornus sericea*) or the blood-twig (*C. sanguinea*).

Somehow surprising:
the pristine white flowers of
Magnolia grandiflora
are followed by a conelike
fruit which bears the
reddest of red seeds (above).
Rosa multiflora is one
of the heaviest producers of
orange-red seed hips
(right), shown along with
muscadine grapes and
autumn witch hazel
(Hamamelis virginiana), all
cut from a sunny hedgerow.

Sedum x rubrotinctum, or Christmas-cheer, is thought to be of garden origin. The succulent leaves are most colorful in winter.

New Zealand flax (*Phormium tenax*), shown *(opposite)* in the tricolored hybrid cultivar 'Maori Sunset,' is potentially one of the most dramatic foliage plants that can be introduced into a cultivated garden. The plants are not frost-hardy, however, so where winter is brisk, arrangements must be made to wheel and containerize. That way they can be coddled inside, airy, never freezing until spring.

A height and spread of 8 to 10 feet (2.5 to 3 m) is not impossible, but half these dimensions is perhaps more likely. The plants need sun, well-drained soil, and, if potted, a container at least 18 inches (46 cm) in diameter. It can be an advantage to have large, colorful-leaved plants like these that are mobile, so that they can be moved in order to be seen in the most flattering light. This is necessary to illuminate the dark purple of 'Purpurea' or the pink-and-purple-striped 'Sundowner.'

Sedums are succulents that come in both cold-hardy and tropical species. One sold as Christmas-cheer, *Sedum x rubrotinctum*, thought to be of garden origin, turns glowing bright red in a mild winter climate. Hardy *S. spurium* 'Dragon's Blood' has red flowers, and purplish leaves.

New Zealand flax (*Phormium*), a member of the Agave family, grows in impressive clumps 8 to 10 feet (2.5 to 3 m) tall and as wide. There are several striped cultivars, such as 'Maori Sunset.' 'Purpureum' is dark purple, 'Sundowner' pink-and-purple.

🌿 *Nidularium innocentii* is a red-leaved bromeliad from the south of Brazil, with foliage variously purplish wine-red to dull crimson.

🌿 Glowing burgundy leaf rosettes of the fireball *Neoregelia* bromeliad grow in full, direct sun over this koi pond in the subtropics. Red-leaved plants usually color up best if they receive strong light.

(5)

complementary color schemes

ℕO DOUBT, RED CAN STAND ALONE IN THE GARDEN, BUT IT can also amount to more on occasion if less is used and a complementary color is added. Here are two examples of how red and blue work together. In the spring scene opposite, rosy pink tulips stand out in a bed of blue pansies and 'Princess Scarlet' dianthus. The vignette above, in a Memphis, Tennessee, dooryard garden, features red hybrid geraniums (*Pelargonium*) in small clay pots (root cramping causes them to bloom more) set at the base of a Colorado blue spruce (*Picea pungens)* growing in a Chinese pot glazed jade-green and cobalt-blue. There are numerous blue conifers, blue-leaved hostas, and 'Jackman's Blue' *Ruta*.

The two photographs here illustrate how different shades of one color get on with those of similar strength in other colors. On this page, red is represented by the modest pink leaves of Joseph's-coat *(Alternanthera)* and wax begonia *(Begonia semperflorens)*, these in turn contrasted with the pale yellow leaves of a different Joseph's-coat and the quiet gray of *Santolina*.

The same palette appears in the garden opposite, but in vivid hues: intense yellow veins in canna leaves, blood-red verbenas, and a barberry with sunflower-yellow leaves.

Bright red flowers can look sensational in the company of red-leaved plants, and in numerous instances nature puts both together: red-leaved and red-flowered dahlias such as 'Bishop of Landorf,' *Lobelia splendens* 'Queen Victoria,' with dark red leaves and bright red flowers, and *Bergenia cordifolia* 'Purpurea,' with red stems, purplish leaves, and magenta flowers.

Set in rows by design, modest pinks (Joseph's-coat and wax begonia), pale yellows (also Joseph's-coat) and silver *Santolina* weave a floral carpet.

This garden of vivid colors grows by a water-lily pond and features striped-leaved cannas, red verbenas, and a golden barberry (*Berberis*), all carefree sun-lovers.

The elegant if somehow
helicopter-like flowers (left)
of the climbing lily
(Gloriosa rothschildiana)
seemingly hurl into the
air from high-reaching stems.
They grow in warm weather
and are choice cut flowers.
The unrelated Gloriosa
daisy (above) is a large-
flowered hybrid of
Rudbeckia hirta that
displays bold balance between
ruby-to-mahogany reds
and similarly intense yellow.

🌿 Rhododendrons and azaleas offer every red imaginable and an alchemistry that miraculously forgives all but the most glaring of apparent color clashes. Part of the magic lies in underplanting the trees and shrubs with something blue, as here: English bluebells (*Hyacinthoides non-scripta*).

Red is a consistently exciting garden theme color, with something new and different to help celebrate each season. The bluish or cool reds, exemplified by the azaleas and rhododendrons pictured (*left*), are often associated with romantic gardens planted with flowers pale to blush pink and set in the company of companions with blooms the color of creamy satin and baby-blue-eyes.

This combination—something red, something creamy white or pale yellow, and something blue—can be scaled up or down in intensity, to suit personal preferences and plant availability.

The "hot" reds seen opposite take their cue from the small but prolific toadflax (*Linaria maroccana*) in a cultivar with maroon-red and golden yellow flowers. The same yellow is repeated by dwarf French marigolds (*Tagetes*); the red of the toadflax is echoed in a lighter, brighter red-pink hybrid geranium (*Pelargonium*) in an outdoor container planting designed to bloom all summer.

sources

Jacques Amand
P.O. Box 59001
Potomac, MD 20859
free catalog; all kinds of bulbs

Amaryllis, Inc.
P.O. Box 318
Baton Rouge, LA 70821
free list; hybrid Hippeastrum

Antique Rose Emporium
Rt. 5, Box 143
Brenham, TX 77833
*catalog $5; old roses; also
perennials, ornamental grasses*

B & D Lilies
330 "P" Street
Port Townsend, WA 98368
catalog $3; garden lilies

Kurt Bluemel
2740 Greene Lane
Baldwin, MD 21013
*catalog $2; ornamental grasses;
perennials*

Bluestone Perennials
7237 Middle Ridge
Madison, OH 44057
free catalog; perennials

Borboleta Gardens
15980 Canby Avenue, Rt. 5
Faribault, MN 55021
*catalog $3; bulbs, tubers, corms,
rhizomes*

Brand Peony Farms
P.O. Box 842
St. Cloud, MN 56302
free catalog; peonies

Breck's
6523 N. Galena Road
Peoria, IL 61632
free catalog; all kinds of bulbs

Briarwood Gardens
14 Gully Lane, R.F.D. 1
East Sandwich, MA 02537
list $1; azaleas, rhododendrons

W. Atlee Burpee Co.
300 Park Avenue
Warminster, PA 18974
*free catalog; seeds, plants, bulbs,
supplies; wide selection*

Busse Gardens
5873 Oliver Avenue S.W.
Cokato, MN 55321
catalog $2; perennials

Canyon Creek Nursery
3527 Dry Creek Road
Oroville, CA 95965
catalog $2; silver-leaved plants

Carroll Gardens
Box 310
Westminster, MD 21158
*catalog $2; perennials, woodies,
herbs*

Coastal Gardens
4611 Socastee Boulevard
Myrtle Beach, SC 29575
catalog $3; perennials

The Cummins Garden
22 Robertsville Road
Marlboro, NJ 07746
*catalog $2; azaleas,
rhododendrons, woodies*

Daylily World
P.O. Box 1612
Sanford, FL 32772
*catalog $5; all kinds of
hemerocallis*

deJager Bulb Co.
Box 2010
South Hamilton, MA 01982
free list; all kinds of bulbs

Tom Dodd's Rare Plants
9131 Holly Street
Semmes, AL 36575
*list $1; trees, shrubs, extremely
select*

Far North Gardens
16785 Harrison Road
Livonia, MI 48154
*catalog $2; primulas, other
perennials*

Howard B. French
Box 565
Pittsfield, VT 05762
free catalog; bulbs

Gardens of the Blue Ridge
Box 10
Pineola, NC 28662
catalog $3; wildflowers and ferns

D.S. George Nurseries
2515 Penfield Road
Fairport, NY 14450
free catalog; clematis

**Glasshouse Works
Greenhouses**
Church Street, Box 97
Stewart, OH 45778
catalog $2; exotics for containers

Greenlee Ornamental Grasses
301 E. Franklin Avenue
Pomona, CA 91766
catalog $5; native and ornamental grasses

Greer Gardens
1280 Goodpasture Is. Rd.
Eugene, OR 97401
catalog $3; uncommon woodies, especially rhododendrons

Grigsby Cactus Gardens
2354 Bella Vista Drive
Vista, CA 92084
catalog $2; cacti and other succulents

Growers Service Co.
10118 Crouse Road
Hartland, MI 48353
list $1; all kinds of bulbs

Heirloom Old Garden Roses
24062 N.E. Riverside Drive
St. Paul, OR 97137
catalog $5; old garden, English, and winter-hardy roses

J.L. Hudson, Seedsman
P.O. Box 1058
Redwood City, CA 94064
catalog $1; nonhybrid flowers, vegetables

Jackson and Perkins
1 Rose Lane
Medford, OR 97501
free catalog; roses, perennials

Kartuz Greenhouses
1408 Sunset Drive
Vista, CA 92083
catalog $2; exotics for containers

Klehm Nursery
Rt. 5, Box 197
Penny Road
South Barrington, IL 60010
catalog $5; peonies, hemerocallis, hostas, perennials

M. & J. Kristick
155 Mockingbird Road
Wellsville, PA 17365
free catalog; conifers

Lamb Nurseries
Rt. 1, Box 460B
Long Beach, WA 98631
catalog $1; perennials

Lauray of Salisbury
432 Undermountain Road, Rt. 41
Salisbury, CT 06068
catalog $2; exotics for containers

Lilypons Water Gardens
6800 Lilypons Road
P.O. Box 10
Buckeystown, MD 21717
catalog $5; aquatics

Limerock Ornamental Grasses
R.D. 1, Box 111
Port Matilda, PA 16870
list $3

Logee's Greenhouses
141 North Street
Danielson, CT 06239
catalog $3; exotics for containers

Louisiana Nursery
Rt. 7, Box 43
Opelousas, LA 70570
catalogs $3-$6; uncommon woodies, perennials

Lowe's Own Root Roses
6 Sheffield Road
Nashua, NH 03062
list $5; old roses

McClure & Zimmerman
Box 368
Friesland, WI 53935
free catalog; all kinds of bulbs

Merry Gardens
Upper Mechanic Street, Box 595
Camden, ME 04843
catalog $2; herbs, Pelargoniums, cultivars of Hedera helix

Milaeger's Gardens
4838 Douglas Avenue
Racine, WI 53402
catalog $1; perennials

Moore Miniature Roses
2519 E. Noble Avenue
Visalia, CA 93292
catalog $1; all kinds of miniature roses

Niche Gardens
1111 Dawson Road
Chapel Hill, NC 27516
catalog $3; perennials

Nor'East Miniature Roses
Box 307
Rowley, MA 01969
free catalog

Oakes Daylilies
8204 Monday Road
Corryton, TN 37721
free catalog; all kinds of hemerocallis

Geo. W. Park Seed Co.
Box 31
Greenwood, SC 29747
free catalog; all kinds of seeds, plants, and bulbs

Roses of Yesterday and Today
802 Brown's Valley Road
Watsonville, CA 95076
catalog $3 third class, $5 first; old roses

Seymour's Selected Seeds
P.O. Box 1346
Sussex, VA 23884
free catalog; English cottage garden seeds

Shady Hill Gardens
821 Walnut Street
Batavia, IL 60510
catalog $2; 800 different Pelargonium

Shady Oaks Nursery
112 10th Ave. S.E.
Waseca, MN 56093
catalog $2.50; hostas, ferns, wildflowers, shrubs

Siskiyou Rare Plant Nursery
2825 Cummings Road
Medford, OR 97501
catalog $2; alpines

Anthony J. Skittone
1415 Eucalyptus
San Francisco, CA 94132
catalog $2; unusual bulbs, especially from South Africa

Sonoma Horticultural Nursery
3970 Azalea Avenue
Sebastopol, CA 95472
catalog $2; azaleas, rhododendrons

Spring Hill Nurseries
110 W. Elm Street
Tipp City, OH 45371
free catalog; perennials, woodies, roses

Steffen Nurseries
Box 184
Fairport, NY 14450
catalog $2; clematis

Sunnybrook Farms Homestead
9448 Mayfield Road
Chesterland, OH 44026
catalog $2; perennials, herbs

Surry Gardens
P.O. Box 145
Surry, ME 04684
free list; perennials, vines, grasses, wild garden

Thompson & Morgan
Box 1308
Jackson, NJ 08527
free catalog; all kinds of seeds

Transplant Nursery
1586 Parkertown Road
Lavonia, GA 30553
catalog $1; azaleas, rhododendrons

Van Engelen, Inc.
Stillbrook Farm
313 Maple Street
Litchfield, CT 06759
free catalog; all kinds of bulbs

Andre Viette Farm & Nursery
Rt. 1, Box 16
Fishersville, VA 22939
catalog $3; perennials, ornamental grasses

Washington Evergreen Nursery
Box 388
Leicester, NC 28748
catalog $2; conifers

Wayside Gardens
One Garden Lane
Hodges, SC 29695
free catalog; all kinds of bulbs, woodies, perennials, vines

We-Du Nursery
Rt. 5, Box 724
Marion, NC 28752
catalog $2; uncommon woodies, perennials

White Flower Farm
Box 50
Litchfield, CT 06759
catalog $5; woodies, perennials, bulbs

Gilbert H. Wild and Son, Inc.
Sarcoxie, MO 64862
catalog $3; perennials, peonies, iris, hemerocallis

Yucca Do
P.O. Box 655
Waller, TX 77484
catalog $2; woodies, perennials

index